Spend a Day in Greater Geneseo / Conesus Lake area

DATES IN THE STATES

A COUPLE TRAVELING THE UNITED STATES ON A BUDGET

I0459343

Mystery Date
Conesus Lake, NY

By Dates in the States

"Our passion is travel, and we want to share our adventures to inspire others to explore the world with their loved ones. Dare to live beyond the box."

Dates in the States

Introduction

Hey there! We're Crystal and Shane, the duo behind Dates in the States, where we share our love for discovering unique adventures, unforgettable moments, and hidden gems across the U.S. Whether you're searching for a fun date idea, a new place to explore, or just a little inspiration, we've got you covered!

Our Mystery Date Books are designed to help couples (and adventurous friends!) shake up their routine and experience the best local spots in a fun, intentional way. Inside, you'll find a curated collection of date ideas. Each one meant to be completed over the course of a single day in a specific neighborhood. All of which are a surprise until you flip the page!

It's like a little challenge to break out of your comfort zone, support local, and make memories that stick. We hope this book helps you laugh more, explore more, and connect more, with each other and with your city. Let the mystery begin!

Here's What To Expect:

In this Mystery Date Book, we're taking you on a playful adventure along the scenic shores of Conesus Lake, exploring lakeside parks, cozy eateries, wineries and cideries, and fun, one-of-a-kind experiences.

Here's what to expect for your day ahead:

Kick off your day at a local fun center. Go-cart racing, anyone? Next, unwind with a relaxing cider & wine tasting, then stretch your legs with a peaceful walk along the lake. Finish your day with a delicious lakeside dinner, perfect for watching the sunset.

This date is all about enjoying the beauty of Conesus Lake, trying new things and making memories!

1st Stop

Minnehan's Fun Center

5601 Big Tree Rd.
Lakeville, NY 14480

Make Minnehans Fun Center your very first stop and jump straight into the fun. If the weather is nice, head outside for go kart racing or a round of mini golf. If it's not cooperating, the arcade inside is packed with games and prizes.

If you're hungry, they do serve breakfast, so feel free to grab a small bite. Just remember that lunch is your next stop. Hours can vary depending on the season, so make sure to check before you go!

Second Stop

3 Legged Pig BBQ Real Pit BBQ

3415 Rochester Rd.
Lakeville, NY 14480

Legged Pig BBQ is hands down our favorite BBQ spot in upstate New York. And we mean that honestly, moving here from Nashville, where good BBQ is everywhere and expectations are high. Finding truly great BBQ up here can be slim pickings, but 3 Legged Pig absolutely tops our list.

This is the perfect place to dig into real pit BBQ, bold flavors, and seriously satisfying comfort food. Come hungry, take your time, and enjoy a no-frills meal that delivers every single time.

Third Stop

OSB Ciderworks

5901 Big Tree Rd.
Lakeville, NY 14480

OSB Ciderworks is hands down one of our favorite cideries in upstate New York. The staff is great, they usually have a dog around and the atmosphere is just plain fun.

Be sure to try their limited edition 3 Pepper Cider. It is seriously to die for. They only seem to have it at certain times of the year, so if you spot it, grab a glass while you can and let us know it's in stock! We're always keeping our eye out for it.

Fourth Stop

Vitale Park

5828 Big Tree Rd.
Lakeville, NY 14480

This stop is totally optional, but worth the views. We highly suggest you take a stroll along the loop at Vitale Park and enjoy beautiful views of Conesus Lake. The trails are easy and scenic, making it a perfect stop for any time of year.

Whether the leaves are changing in fall, flowers are blooming in spring, or the water sparkles in summer, Vitale Park offers a peaceful, refreshing moment to stretch your legs and take in the natural beauty around you.

P.S. Another park you may enjoy is Conesus Lake Inlet at the other side of the lake if you have time!

Fifth Stop

Deer Run Winery

3772 W Lake Rd.

Geneseo, NY 14454

This is why we wanted you to take a walk. To break up the cider tasting to move into a wine tasting. Deer Run Winery has some delicious wines so we had to try and fit them in this book!

Treat yourselves to one of their amazing flights or try their fun and refreshing wine slushies. Each flavor is crafted to be playful and full of taste, making it a perfect way to explore a variety of options. Our favorite is their Cherry Cocoa dessert wine or Max Black that pairs well with Reese's - trust us!

Final Stop

Beachcomber

5909 W Lake Rd.

Conesus, NY 14435

If any place on Conesus Lake screams lake vibes, it's the Beachcomber. Come for the food, stay for the view. It's perfect any time of year. On a warm day, grab a seat at the bar or under the tents outside. In the winter, cozy up inside and enjoy their delicious seafood dishes. Watch the sunset, listen to live music, or soak up the lively bar scene.

And if you need a place to stay, they also have rooms available right on the lake.

Add Your Photos

Your Memory

Use this space to record a favorite moment

Thank you for joining us on this mystery date adventure! We hope you've enjoyed the delightful experiences and memorable moments we've crafted just for you around Conesus Lake, NY.

But the adventure doesn't stop here! Keep exploring exciting mystery dates in other cities and uncover new experiences across the U.S. by visiting our website, DatesintheStates.com. There, you can purchase both physical copies and digital downloads of our mystery date books.

Plus, don't miss out on our Mystery Date Book Club, where you can receive a brand-new mystery date book every month!
Tag us in your date photos on social media! @datesinthestates

About the Creators

Crystal, the writer and creator, is a storyteller at heart. When she's not uncovering hidden gems for the next date night idea, she runs her own digital marketing company, helping small businesses improve their content marketing, increase visibility in their communities, and streamline their online presence.
Visit: crystalstatskey.com

Shane, her husband and partner in adventure, is a dedicated personal trainer and the owner of Beekstar Fitness in Irondequoit, NY. He specializes in working with clients who have limited mobility, helping them build muscle and focus on pain areas so they can regain strength and confidence in their daily lives.
Visit: beekstarfitness.com

Crystal and Shane have explored every U.S. state except Alaska (coming soon!) and are now visiting countries in alphabetical order. Whether road-tripping or curating Mystery Date experiences, they're always chasing their next adventure.

Local Love

A few local gems in the area worth exploring on your next date.

SCENT AND STONE HOLISTIC ENERGIES

METAPHYSICAL SUPPLY STORE

4550 MILLENNIUM DR, GENESEO, NY 14454

LEISURE'S RESTAURANT

GREAT BREAKFAST & LUNCH SPOT

6001 BIG TREE RD, LAKEVILLE, NY 14480

EMBER WOODFIRE GRILL

DELICIOUS DINNER

21 LIVONIA STATION, LIVONIA, NY 14487

Want to see your business here?
See the next page for details on
how to join!

Want to be featured?

MYSTERY DATE BOOK PACKAGES

—

Are you a small business looking to reach new customers? Feature your business in our next Mystery Date Book! Choose from our partnership packages below to connect with couples seeking unique experiences and exclusive deals.

Package One
LOCAL LOVE LISTING

—

A quick shoutout to show you're part of the neighborhood vibe.

Listed in the "Local Love" section of your designated neighborhood date book

Includes business name, address, and social link

Optional: Offer a small promo (e.g., 10% off for book holders)

1 social media shout-out when the book launches

Package Two
FEATURE STOP

—

You're not just a business—you're part of the experience.

Marked as a "Must-Stop" on a Mystery Date

Full-page feature in the book with your story, offerings and photo

Includes 1 social media feature — a dedicated post and story highlighting your business

Note: To ensure each feature is genuine and experience-based, we require a hosted visit prior to inclusion.

Package Three
PARTNER & SELLER

—

Be the spot and the source.

Everything in Tier 2

PLUS: Option to sell the Mystery Date Books at your location

Includes a bulk purchase of 10 books (yours to price + sell)

Keep 100% of the profits from in-store sales

Bonus: Have a featured "sponsored by" page and listed as an official pickup location in our promotions

Contact us for pricing. Prices subject to change.

Feel free to reach us at any time by sending us an email to say hi and to learn more! We look forward to hearing from you.

| www.datesinthestates.com | datesinthestatesblog@gmail.com |

Sponsors & Affiliates

Our sponsors and affiliates help make our adventures possible! Explore the amazing brands and businesses that support our community.

Wanderful

Wanderful is a global community for women who love to travel. Connect, explore, and join a local hub near you!

Join our Book Club!

Join our Mystery Date Book Club and be part of a travel-inspired community, discovering unique local adventures together!

HomeExchange

HomeExchange lets you swap homes with travelers worldwide for authentic, affordable stays. Join today and travel differently!

Shop our books at a store near you!

Little Button Craft
658 South Ave.
Rochester, NY 14620

The Pawsitive Cat Cafe
120 East Ave. Ste 100
Rochester, NY 14604

Yesterday's Muse Books
32 West Main St.
Webster, NY 14580

Nashville Souvenirs
2613 McGavock Pk,
Nashville, TN 37214

Music Valley Antiques
16 Music Valley Dr.
Nashville, TN 37214

Barnes & Noble
1 Walden Galleria g113,
Buffalo, NY 14225

Abundance Food Co-op
571 South Ave,
Rochester, NY 14620

Union Tavern
4565 Culver Rd,
Irondequoit, NY 14622

DATES IN THE STATES

A COUPLE TRAVELING THE UNITED
STATES ON A BUDGET

🌐

datesinthestates.com

✉️

datesinthestatesblog@gmail.com

📍

Based in Rochester, NY

CONNECT WITH US ON SOCIAL!
@DATESINTHESTATES